What Is a Presidential Election?

WITH ACTIVITIES,
STICKERS,
AND A POSTER!

by Douglas Yacka
illustrations by Robert Squier and others

Penguin Workshop

PENGUIN WORKSHOP
An Imprint of Penguin Random House LLC, New York

ISBN 9780593095614   10 9 8 7 6 5 4 3 2 1

Contents

What Is a Presidential Election?

Every four years, the people of the United States of America choose a president to lead the country. All citizens who are eighteen or older may vote in the election.

Serving as the president of the United States is probably the hardest job that there is. Often called the "leader of the free world," the president has many powers, including being Commander in Chief—that means head of all branches of the US military. The president also decides whether to approve laws that have been passed by Congress.

VOTE
HERE

President Andrew Jackson

The president makes decisions that can affect the lives of billions of people around the world—for example, deciding whether the United States will join in worldwide agreements on important issues such as the environment.

The choice of whom to vote for is very important. Of all the people who could vote in the 2016 presidential election, guess how many did? Circle the answer you think is right.

81%   69%   58%   47%   33%

ANSWER: It's 58%—only a little more than half of the people who could vote actually did.

The 2020 presidential election is under way. Maybe you are keeping up with it by following the news. Maybe you've heard your parents or other family members talking about it.

At first, more than twenty Democrats entered the race. They competed with one another for the chance to run against the current president, Republican Donald J. Trump. He wants to get reelected for another four years. Because of the coronavirus pandemic, this will be an unusual election season. Still, on November 3, 2020, the American people will decide whom to send to the White House.

President Donald J. Trump

What do you think are the most important qualities a president should have? Make a list below.

1 _____

2 _____

3 _____

4 _____

5 _____

6 _____

7 _____

8 _____

9 _____

10 _____

Chapter 1
Checks and Balances

Sure, the president is very powerful. But the president doesn't hold all the power.

In the United States, there are three branches of government. Each branch makes sure the other two aren't overstepping their use of power. This is known as a system of "checks and balances."

The president and their advisors make up the executive branch.

Congress makes up the legislative branch. Congress includes the Senate—with two senators from every state—and the House of Representatives. The number of representatives a state has depends on how many people live there.

It is Congress who passes national laws—laws that all states must obey.

How many representatives does your state have?_____

Who are your senators in Congress? _____

_____

Which state do you think has the biggest
number of representatives? _____

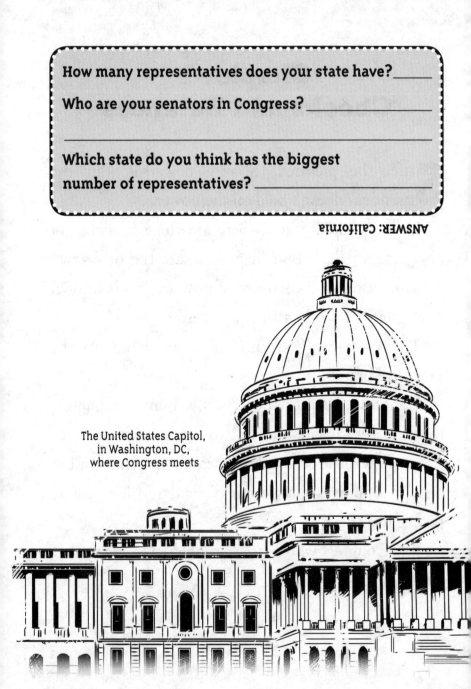

The United States Capitol,
in Washington, DC,
where Congress meets

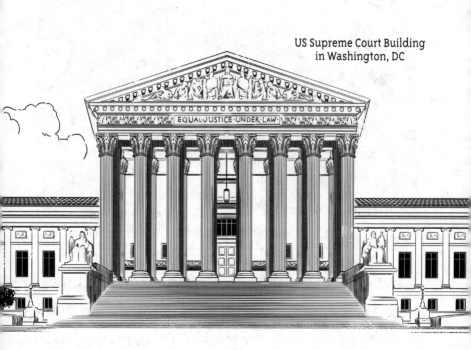

US Supreme Court Building
in Washington, DC

EQUAL JUSTICE UNDER LAW

The third branch of our government is the judicial branch. It's made up of all the courts in the country. The US Supreme Court is the highest court in the land. There are nine justices (judges) on the Supreme Court who serve for life, or until they choose to retire. That means there aren't openings very often.

Who gets to select judges to sit on the Supreme Court and other federal courts? The president does.

US Supreme Court, March 2020: Elena Kagan, Samuel A. Alito Jr.,
Ruth Bader Ginsburg, Brett M. Kavanaugh, John G. Roberts Jr. (Chief Justice)

But the Senate votes on whether to confirm those judges. If they don't give their approval, the president has to nominate someone else. In his first two years in office, President Trump appointed two justices after one died and another retired.

Clarence Thomas, Stephen G. Breyer, Sonia Sotomayor, Neil M. Gorsuch

What can a president do?

	TRUE	FALSE
1. Sign bills from Congress into law	☐	☐
2. Veto (reject) a bill from Congress, although Congress can overrule the president's veto	☐	☐
3. Make laws	☐	☐
4. Serve as Commander in Chief for the United States military	☐	☐
5. Nominate justices to the Supreme Court	☐	☐
6. Nominate members of the cabinet (advisors), such as Secretary of State	☐	☐
7. Fire senators or representatives	☐	☐
8. Change the Constitution	☐	☐
9. Deal with the leaders of other countries	☐	☐
10. Represent the American people all around the world	☐	☐
11. Declare a national emergency if citizens are in danger	☐	☐
12. Decide how to spend money collected in taxes	☐	☐
13. Run for a third term	☐	☐
14. Grant pardons if they feel someone was wrongfully convicted of a crime	☐	☐

ANSWERS: 1. True; 2. True; 3. False; 4. True; 5. True; 6. True; 7. False; 8. False; 9. True; 10. True; 11. True; 12. False; 13. False; 14. True

Chapter 2
To Run or Not to Run?

Why does someone run for president? For lots of reasons!

One person might see the need for many big changes—changes in how much people pay in taxes, changes to protect the environment, changes in how people get health care. Another person might want to keep things the way they are or even return the country to a time they think was better.

There's one thing, however, they all have in common—they each believe that they are the best person to improve the lives of US citizens. That sure takes a lot of confidence!

To run for president, a person must . . .

	TRUE	FALSE
1. Be born a citizen of the United States	☐	☐
2. Know all the words to "The Star-Spangled Banner"	☐	☐
3. Be at least thirty-five years old	☐	☐
4. Speak at least two foreign languages	☐	☐
5. Have lived in the United States for at least fourteen years	☐	☐
6. Not have served two previous four-year terms as president	☐	☐

ANSWERS: 1. True; 2. False; 3. True; 4. False; 5. True; 6. True

More than 250 million US citizens will be eligible to vote in the 2020 election. So people hoping to become president have a lot of voters to convince!

Some presidential candidates may already be well-known to the public. Maybe they are current or former senators or governors who have been in the news for years. Joe Biden had been both a senator from Delaware and vice president under Barack Obama before he decided to run for president in the 2020 election. Often a vice president will run for president once the president he served with can't run again.

President Barack Obama and Vice President Joe Biden

If the president resigns, dies in office, or becomes so sick they can't carry on the job anymore, the vice president becomes president. Because of this, the vice president—also known as the "VP" or "veep"—is sometimes jokingly referred to as the "president in waiting."

It is true that for some vice presidents, the job has been little more than a title. Others, however, have had strong influence in the executive branch. They have helped make important decisions and provided presidents with advice and assistance.

The vice president is also the president of the Senate. There are one hundred members of the US Senate. If a vote comes to a 50–50 tie, the veep casts the deciding vote.

Gerald Ford became president when Richard Nixon resigned the presidency.

Occasionally, a presidential candidate has never been in politics before. Ulysses S. Grant was a military general who had never held elected office. Donald Trump was a businessman and reality TV star.

★ ★ ★ ★ ★ ★ ★

Who would you like to see run for president? Why?

_____

_____

_____

_____

_____

_____

_____

_____

_____

_____

_____

_____

★ ★ ★ ★ ★ ★ ★

Some candidates—even those already in politics—are mostly unknown to the public until they declare they're running. For example, in the 2020 race, Pete Buttigieg had been the mayor of South Bend, Indiana, and Tulsi Gabbard was a US representative in Congress from Hawaii. Many Americans did not know their names before the early Democratic debates in the 2020 race.

Senator Kamala Harris appeared on *The Late Show with Stephen Colbert.*

Before entering the race, many presidential hopefuls will form what is called an "exploratory committee." During this time, they will test the waters by traveling around the country to talk (and listen) to people about different issues and to let the public get to know them. The exploratory committee also begins raising money in case the person decides to run.

The easiest way to reach out to the public is through social media, posting opinions in real time based on the news of the day. The candidates will also appear on TV, usually on news programs and late-night or daytime talk shows.

Cable news channels like CNN, Fox News, and MSNBC devote much of their time to covering the race even in its very early stages. Pundits (political experts) will appear on these networks to promote their candidates and say what is wrong with the other political party.

Even presidents must campaign if they want a second term. For instance, Donald Trump was the president in 2020. That meant he was the incumbent. He campaigned for a second term so he could keep his job until January 2025. That's when the president who is elected in 2020 will finish their term. (Presidents can only be elected to two four-year terms.)

Incumbents enjoy some big advantages in an election. To begin with, they are already well-known to the public. The current president also has an easier time raising money for the campaign. They take credit for good things that are happening. And think of all of the free publicity they get simply from being in the news every single day.

BREAKING NEWS

TRUMP SPEAKS TO THE PRESS

LIVE

A president is not guaranteed the nomination, however. In 1856, Democrats chose James Buchanan as their candidate over the current president, Franklin Pierce. And sometimes a president—for example, Lyndon B. Johnson in 1968—decides not to run again.

Leading the Way

Until Barack Obama in 2008, all US presidents had been white men. Here are just a few of the people who broke down barriers in running for president.

⭐ Victoria Woodhull (1872): First woman candidate (forty-eight years before women were allowed to vote in the United States!)

⭐ Frederick Douglass (1888): First black candidate

⭐ Al Smith (1928): First Catholic

⭐ Hiram Fong (1964): First Asian-American

⭐ Shirley Chisholm (1972): First black woman

Shirley Chisholm

⭐ Ben Fernandez (1980): First Hispanic

⭐ Hillary Clinton (2016): First woman to be the candidate of a major political party

⭐ Pete Buttigieg (2020): First openly gay man

The youngest president elected to office was John F. Kennedy in 1960 at forty-three years old. The oldest to be elected was Donald Trump in 2016 at age seventy.

Chapter 3
Ready, Set,
Start Campaigning!

In recent years, candidates have been entering the presidential race earlier and earlier. It wasn't always like this.

In January 1960, Democratic senator John F. Kennedy announced that he would run for president. The election was that November—only ten months away. In the 2020 election, Democratic senator Elizabeth Warren of Massachusetts announced that she was running in February 2019 —almost twenty-one months before Election Day.

Elizabeth Warren

Picking a platform

The candidates' ideas and opinions on important issues are known as their platforms. Rank the following issues (1–6) in order of their importance to you. If any aren't important to you, put an X in the box by those issues:

☐ Better education

☐ Protection of the environment

☐ Free college tuition

☐ Good, affordable medical care

☐ Lower taxes

☐ Cutting costs for government programs

☐ Equal rights and protections for all Americans

For more than 150 years, the Democrats and Republicans have been the two major political parties in the United States. During this time, all presidents have belonged to one of those parties. For instance, Barack Obama was a Democratic senator from Illinois and George W. Bush was the Republican governor of Texas before they were elected to the highest office in the nation.

Before he held political office, Donald Trump had once been a Democrat. He thought that party's

Governor of Texas George W. Bush with supporters during his successful 2000 presidential election campaign

ideas best matched his own. However, by the time he decided in 2015 to run for president, he felt his ideas and opinions were most in line with those of the Republican Party. So he ran as a Republican.

Many Americans don't consider themselves either a Democrat or a Republican. Instead, in every election, they vote based on which candidate they like best. These voters are often referred to as "independents."

Which way do you lean? Answer "Yes" or "No."

YES	NO	
☐	☐	1. I believe more tax money should be spent on education and improving schools.
☐	☐	2. I believe in lower taxes so people will have more money in their pockets.
☐	☐	3. I think there should be strict laws making sure businesses can't pollute the environment.
☐	☐	4. I believe the government should stay out of people's business as much as possible.
☐	☐	5. I believe that the government should make affordable health care available to all Americans.
☐	☐	6. I believe that more money needs to be spent on our military.
☐	☐	7. I believe in higher taxes for wealthy people and big businesses to pay for government-sponsored programs like school lunch programs for children whose families don't have much money.

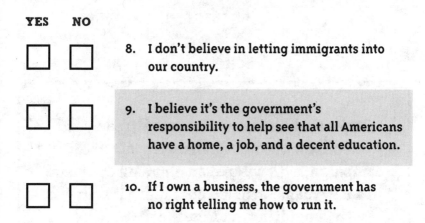

YES	NO	
☐	☐	8. I don't believe in letting immigrants into our country.
☐	☐	9. I believe it's the government's responsibility to help see that all Americans have a home, a job, and a decent education.
☐	☐	10. If I own a business, the government has no right telling me how to run it.

★ ★ ★ ★ ★ ★ ★

If you answered "Yes" to more of the odd-numbered questions, you agree with many ideas held by Democrats. If you answered "Yes" to more even-numbered questions, then you fall more on the Republican side. Or maybe you fall somewhere in between. Many Americans do.

Ask grown-up family members if they would be willing to answer these questions. Find out what kind of government they think is best.

The Republican Party is symbolized by an elephant. During Abraham Lincoln's 1860 campaign, a drawing of an elephant appeared in a newspaper article about him. Lincoln was a Republican, and the elephant was meant to convey strength.

The Democratic Party is symbolized by a donkey. This goes back to Andrew Jackson's 1828 campaign. Jackson's opponents called him a donkey because of his stubborn ways, but Jackson didn't care. In fact, he put the donkey on his campaign posters.

Chapter 4
Show Us the Money!

Money plays an important role in any campaign. Without it, a candidate really has no hope of winning.

In the beginning of a campaign, the US government provides money to candidates to match donations they receive from individuals. These are called matching funds. US taxpayers may choose to contribute three dollars to support this program when they file their yearly taxes.

But modern presidential campaigns are so expensive, and matching funds won't pay for everything. In the 2016 election, Donald Trump's campaign raised $647 million. Democratic candidate Hillary

US tax form

Clinton's campaign raised nearly $1.2 billion.

Any US citizen can donate to a presidential campaign. Even kids can! In the 2016 election, Senator Bernie Sanders of Vermont tried to become the Democrats' presidential nominee. He received over 2.5 million donations—the average amount was twenty-seven dollars. Still, the donations added up, and Bernie Sanders became a serious contender for the nomination that Hillary Clinton eventually won. Bernie ran again in 2020. As of March of the election year, he had received more than five million donations!

On the other hand, wealthy people are often eager to contribute a lot of money to the candidate of their choice. However, there is a limit to the amount one person can give. This is to make sure no single person has too much influence over the candidate.

Of course, some wealthy people can run for president and spend as much of their own money as they want. Billionaire and former New York City mayor Michael Bloomberg ran to be the Democratic nominee in 2020. He spent $900 million before withdrawing from the race after just three months.

There are ways to get around the donation limit besides giving money to your own campaign. Instead of giving money directly to the candidate, people or big businesses can donate to a political action committee, or PAC.

A PAC is not officially part of a campaign. PACs spend their money on advertisements and promotions for the candidate of their choice. So, in a way, they are acting as if they are part of the campaign.

★　★　★　★　★　★　★

Do you think this system is fair?
Write a sentence or two to back up your opinion.

_____

_____

_____

_____

_____

★　★　★　★　★　★　★

The biggest political action committees are called Super PACs. There's no limit on how much can be given—a donation could be millions of dollars!

Super PACs have only existed since 2010. During the 2012 election, Super PACs supporting Republican challenger Mitt Romney far outspent those in favor of the incumbent, President Obama. In 2016, Super PACs supporting Hillary Clinton raised over $200 million, more than twice what Super PACs supporting Donald Trump spent.

Mitt Romney in 2012

Why is it so expensive to run a campaign? One reason is all the people who need to be hired.

One of the most important jobs is that of the campaign manager. This person oversees the many other people who are part of the campaign. There are campaign offices to be set up in each state. Money to raise. People to help get out the vote on Election Day. It is the campaign manager's job to keep all these things organized.

Campaign managers also work with campaign strategists. They come up with a strategy—a game plan—to win. For example, they figure out in which states to spend the most time and money.

Donald Trump's 2016 campaign manager, Kellyanne Conway, the first woman to run a Republican presidential campaign

A campaign must also have a communications director. This person handles anything related to media, which is the many ways that information about a candidate is spread, including ads on TV, radio, the internet, and social media sites like Facebook and Twitter. Communications directors often help the candidate write speeches or statements that are given to the press and released to the public.

If you had a million bucks . . .

If you were a communications director and had a million dollars to spend in one week, how would you divide it up?

___% TV ads

___% Radio ads

___% Social media ads

___% Signs for people's front lawns

___% Bumper stickers

___% Pins and buttons

Some of the most important people in a campaign are the volunteers. These people aren't paid. They devote their time and energy because they believe in the candidate and their ideas.

They call and text voters, asking for their support. They go door-to-door through neighborhoods to convince as many people as possible to vote for

their candidate. They may ask for donations to the campaign. Or for people to get involved in other ways—like becoming volunteers themselves! They encourage people who aren't registered to vote to do so and organize carpools to drive people to vote if they need transportation on Election Day. They donate food and supplies to campaign offices—sometimes they even clean them! Every little bit helps. To keep things organized, a campaign will have a main volunteer coordinator to assign these jobs.

Barack Obama's 2008 campaign had over two million volunteers. Many were first-time voters.

One of the main reasons Election Day is held in the beginning of November is that for much of US history, most citizens were farmers. The election needed to be after the busy harvest season but before the harsh winter.

Chapter 5
On the Campaign Trail

During the months before the general election in November, each political party holds state elections called primaries. (In some states, they are called caucuses.) For example, Democrats in Minnesota will pick which of the Democratic candidates they think is best.

Unlike the general election, primaries and caucuses are not all held on the same day. Each state picks its own date. "Primary season" begins in February of the election year and runs through June.

One way that candidates introduce themselves and their ideas to the country is through televised debates with the other candidates in the race. These debates start early so voters can better choose whom to back in their state's primary. During the debates, candidates come together to answer tough questions about how they would run the government.

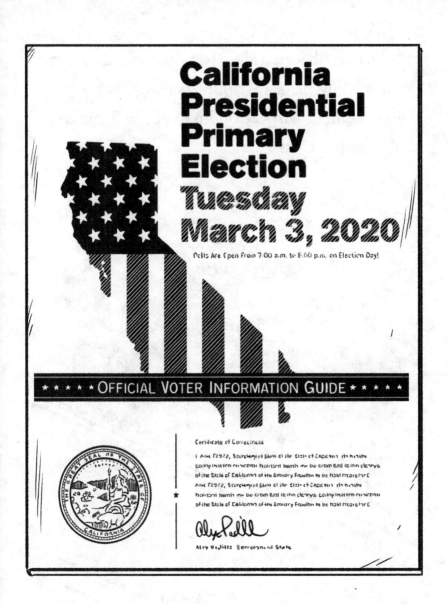

California **Presidential Primary Election** Tuesday March 3, 2020

Polls Are Open From 7:00 a.m. to 8:00 p.m. on Election Day!

★ ★ ★ ★ OFFICIAL VOTER INFORMATION GUIDE ★ ★ ★ ★

In the 2016 election, seventeen men and women, including Donald Trump, were running for president on the Republican side. The Republican primary debates really helped Trump increase his following. Before them, few expected him to be the Republicans' choice for president.

Melania Trump with Donald Trump

There will still be Republican primary elections in 2020, but there won't be any Republican debates. That's because President Trump is all but certain to be his party's nominee again.

Democrats, however, debated other Democrats. Early in the 2020 election, the Democrats' debate stage was very full. There were so many candidates, in fact, they all couldn't fit on one stage. So the first two debates were held over two nights, with the group of candidates split into two groups of ten. A third debate, the largest in history, featured twelve candidates onstage. But by the fourth debate in January 2020, the number was down to six. By the eleventh debate, in March, only two candidates remained.

Who's in the running?

Check the names of the two Democratic candidates for president who were still in the race at the time of the March 15, 2020, debate. Put an "X" by the names of people who have dropped out. (One person on the list was never a candidate! Can you spot who it was?)

- [ ] Elizabeth Warren
- [ ] Cory Booker
- [ ] Kamala Harris
- [ ] Beto O'Rourke
- [ ] Bernie Sanders
- [ ] Pete Buttigieg
- [ ] Joe Biden
- [ ] Amy Klobuchar
- [ ] Kirsten Gillibrand
- [ ] Steve Bullock

Minnesota senator
Amy Klobuchar

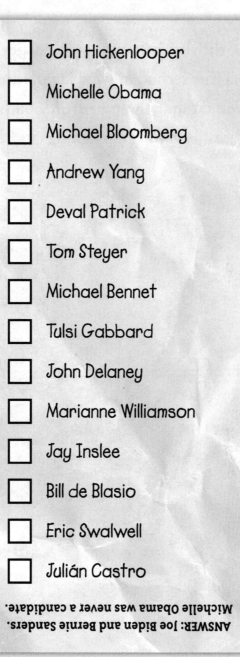

☐ John Hickenlooper

☐ Michelle Obama

☐ Michael Bloomberg

☐ Andrew Yang

☐ Deval Patrick

☐ Tom Steyer

☐ Michael Bennet

☐ Tulsi Gabbard

☐ John Delaney

☐ Marianne Williamson

☐ Jay Inslee

☐ Bill de Blasio

☐ Eric Swalwell

☐ Julián Castro

**ANSWER: Joe Biden and Bernie Sanders.
Michelle Obama was never a candidate.**

In 2020, the first battle for both parties was in the state of Iowa, the second in New Hampshire, with the third in Nevada and the fourth in South Carolina. So candidates began campaigning in these states very early on.

NEVADA

The winner of each contest gets a head start in the race because they become better known to people in other states before those states vote in their primaries.

IOWA

NEW HAMPSHIRE

SOUTH CAROLINA

Until Barack Obama won in Iowa in 2008, many people did not know who he was. Obama's victory moved him further into the national spotlight. He eventually became the Democratic presidential nominee and won the general election.

Chapter 6
Party Time!

After the states have held their primaries and caucuses, it usually becomes clear who will win the nomination and run in the general election. Still, the official announcement isn't made until a presidential convention is held, a weeklong event that usually happens in July or August. Conventions are large events held in stadiums or arenas. However, with worries about the coronavirus pandemic, the 2020 conventions might look different from previous conventions. The 2020 Democratic National Convention was scheduled to be held in mid-August in Milwaukee, Wisconsin. The Republican National Convention was scheduled for the end of August in Charlotte, North Carolina.

Aside from nominating a candidate, conventions are like big, entertaining pep rallies where politicians give speeches and people wave banners and applaud like crazy.

Who gets to go to these conventions?

Besides famous politicians, the most important people are each state's delegates. The number of delegates from each state is determined by the state's population. As a group they are called a delegation. And as a group, they will cast their vote all together for a nominee. (There are two states, however—Maine and Nebraska—that can split their vote.)

Many other people attend the conventions as well. Thousands of special guests, including campaign workers and big donors, are invited.

The presidential nominee, of course, will be there. (There's an acceptance speech to give!) And the candidate for vice president will also attend.

There are a number of reasons why a presidential candidate might select a particular running mate. A younger candidate may want an older VP so that someone with more experience in government will be part of the ticket. Or an older candidate may choose a younger running mate who appeals to younger voters. The presidential nominee might also choose someone of a different gender or background, or from a different part of the country, to connect with citizens across the map.

Many presidents and vice presidents don't know each other well before running together. The decision has more to do with a plan to win the election than with the chance to form a lifelong friendship.

In 1984, Democrat Walter Mondale chose Congresswoman Geraldine Ferraro to be his running mate, the first time in US history a woman was on the presidential ticket for a major party. (They lost to incumbent President Ronald Reagan and his vice president, George H. W. Bush.)

Senator John McCain, the Republican nominee in 2008, with his vice presidential running mate, Alaska governor Sarah Palin

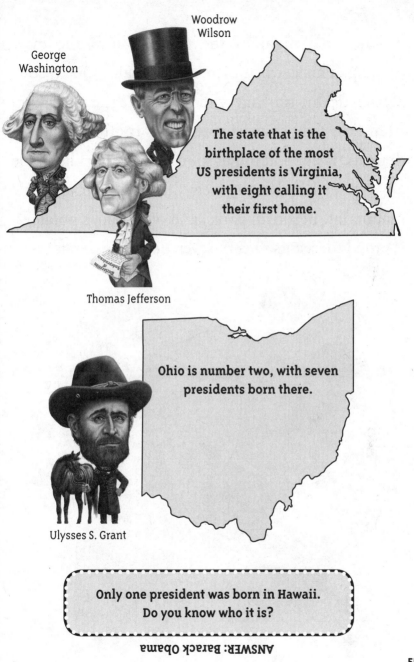

George Washington

Woodrow Wilson

The state that is the birthplace of the most US presidents is Virginia, with eight calling it their first home.

Thomas Jefferson

Ohio is number two, with seven presidents born there.

Ulysses S. Grant

Only one president was born in Hawaii. Do you know who it is?

ANSWER: Barack Obama

55

The final night of the convention is the most exciting. This is when there's a "roll call." One by one alphabetically, starting with Alabama, the delegation from each state casts its votes. This is often done in a dramatic fashion. It might sound something like, "The great state of Idaho, the Gem State, home of majestic mountains, beautiful parks, and our famous potatoes, is proud to cast its twenty-seven delegate votes for . . ."

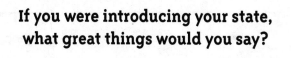

If you were introducing your state, what great things would you say?

Smoke-Filled Rooms

The roll call of delegates is fairly new to the nomination of a candidate. Until the second half of the twentieth century, party leaders met in secret in what were called "smoke-filled rooms," since the deals made were not visible to the public. These men would pick the candidate of their choice, an undemocratic process known as the "old boss system." Many Americans recognized this as unfair to the many people who had voted in primaries. At the 1968 Democratic National Convention, Hubert Humphrey was the candidate, although he had not run in any primaries. Riots broke out, and by the next presidential convention, state delegate votes were finally acknowledged.

At the end of the roll call, the votes are added up, and the winner is now officially the party's nominee for president. (Sometimes, no candidate is the winner, so there is a second roll call, with some states changing their votes.) Finally, the nominee makes an acceptance speech. The speech is a chance to inspire all the members of the party, to rally them for the final months of the campaign, and to state the nominee's vision for America's future. Since many Americans watch the conventions on TV, it is an opportunity for the nominee to connect with undecided voters across the country.

At the end of their speech, the nominee's family will join them onstage, along with the vice presidential nominee and their family. The arena will erupt in cheers. Confetti and balloons will drop from above. Then the convention ends.

But the Democratic and Republican nominees won't stop campaigning until Election Day.

Chapter 7
"I Like Ike"

Once the parties have their nominees, the race is on! The candidates will now crisscross the country and make their case to the American people. Their campaigns will create catchy slogans to help them capture voters' attention.

A political slogan is a short, uplifting phrase that voters will remember. Barack Obama's slogan was "Yes, we can." Hillary Clinton's was "Stronger together."

In 2016, Donald Trump's slogan was "Make America great again." People at his campaign rallies wore red baseball caps with those words on them. It was such a popular slogan that many supporters still wore their red hats to his rallies for the 2020 election.

Presidential Slogans of the Past

★ Warren G. Harding, 1920: "Return to normalcy"
World War I had just ended, and Americans wanted to go back to their regular lives.

★ Calvin Coolidge, 1924: "Keep cool with Coolidge"

★ Dwight (Ike) Eisenhower, 1952: "I like Ike"

★ Herbert Hoover, 1928: "A chicken in every pot and a car in every garage"
Unfortunately, Hoover's promise was not kept. In 1929, the stock market crashed and plunged our country into the Great Depression.

★ Ronald Reagan, 1984: "It's morning again in America"
The economy was improving after Reagan's first term.

The campaign logo is a design to remind people about the candidate. It is often the candidate's name or initials written boldly, usually in patriotic red, white, and blue, the colors of the US flag. Supporters post signs with logos and slogans on their front lawns. They wear T-shirts, pins, and hats with the logo. They put bumper stickers on their cars. They post the logo on social media. It seems that logos are just about everywhere you look during a presidential race!

Check off the places where you've seen presidential-election logos and slogans:

☐ TV ads
☐ Storefront windows
☐ Front lawns
☐ People's clothing
☐ Bumper stickers

What would your slogan be?
Write it on the bumper sticker.

Make some campaign logos for yourself.
Draw them in the buttons.

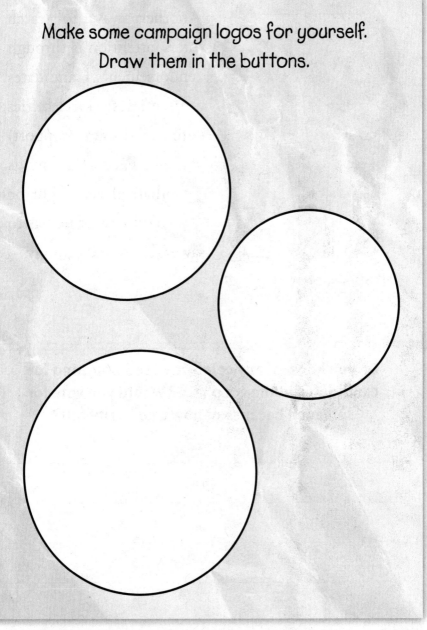

Another way to catch voters' attention is through endorsements. Candidates sometimes ask celebrities to endorse (support) them. Fans of a famous football player might be swayed by what he has to say and vote accordingly.

Superstar couple Beyoncé and Jay-Z with Hillary Clinton, 2016

★ ★ ★ ★ ★ ★ ★

Do you know of any celebrities campaigning for candidates in the 2020 race? Would you vote for someone because of how a celebrity felt?

_____

_____

_____

_____

★ ★ ★ ★ ★ ★ ★

Well-known, popular politicians will also endorse candidates. Many times, politicians who competed against the nominee during the primaries will now declare their support for them. Senator Bernie Sanders endorsed Hillary Clinton in 2016 after he lost the Democratic nomination to her; likewise, Republican senator Ted Cruz endorsed Donald Trump.

Texas senator Ted Cruz calling voters for Donald Trump

Chapter 8
The Electoral College

The candidates work hard for every vote they get. When all the votes are counted on Election Day, whoever receives the most wins what is called the "popular vote." But believe it or not, whoever wins the most votes does not necessarily become president. Although every vote counts, the way a presidential election is ultimately decided is different than you might expect.

More than two centuries ago, when only about four million people lived in the United States, our country's founders created something called the Electoral College.

The Electoral College isn't a school. It isn't even a place. It is a group of people called electors who cast their vote for president after the votes on Election Day come in.

The Founding Fathers

Electors don't actually get elected themselves. They are chosen by their political parties in their home states. Each state gets a certain number of electors, depending on how many members of Congress are from that state. California, the state with the most people living in it, has fifty-five electoral votes. Wyoming, the state with the lowest population, has three. Counting all fifty states, there are 538 electors, so a candidate must win a majority—270 electoral votes—to land the presidency.

How do the electors decide whom to vote for? It depends on who wins the popular vote in their states.

If more people in Arizona vote for Donald Trump than for any other candidate, then the state's eleven electors will all cast their votes for him. (Two states, Nebraska and Maine, can split up their electoral votes.)

When the Electoral College was created, Americans—especially people living outside of urban areas—were much less informed about the candidates. Our founders wanted to ensure that citizens in less populated areas were represented in the presidential vote as well as those in big cities.

Some people believe that the Electoral College is unfair and unnecessary, since people in all parts of the country now have access to information about the candidates and the important issues facing the country. They think that the candidate who wins the most votes should become president, the same as in any other election for public office. Others argue that the Electoral College still provides a more equal representation between areas of the country with higher populations and those with fewer people.

Most recently, in the 2016 election, Democratic candidate Hillary Clinton received about three million more votes than Donald Trump but still lost the election. How many other times in US history has a candidate lost the popular vote but won the electoral vote, the vote that determines who wins the presidency?

ANSWER: Four times. 1824 John Quincy Adams; 1876 Rutherford B. Hayes; 1888 Benjamin Harrison; 2000 George W. Bush

Which system do you think is fairer?
The popular vote or the electoral vote? Why?

_____

_____

_____

_____

_____

_____

_____

_____

Chapter 9
Red, Blue, and Purple

Some states, such as New York and California, are called "blue states." That's the color that represents the Democratic Party. They are called blue because the majority of people in those states vote for the Democratic presidential candidate nearly all the time.

Other states, such as Tennessee and South Dakota, tend to be won by Republicans. Those states are called "red states," the color of the Republican Party.

Mount Rushmore, South Dakota

And some states are called "purple states" because it's hard to predict which party will win there. Many people will vote Republican (red) and many will vote Democrat (blue). (Remember, red and blue make purple.)

Unpredictable "purple states" are known as swing states. These states can *swing* an election either way. This is why candidates will spend much of their time campaigning in swing states—because winning there may win them the presidency. Historically, some swing states are Florida, Ohio, Pennsylvania, and Colorado.

President George W. Bush campaigning
for reelection in Florida, 2004

Look up the results of the 2016 election.
What "color" was your state?
What about in 2012? Or in 1984?

Chapter 10
Homestretch

Have you ever watched Olympic runners or a NASCAR race? You can usually see who is in the lead moment by moment. In a political race, this isn't possible. So campaigns rely on polls (surveys of voters). Polls are taken by newspapers, TV stations, news organizations, universities, and private polling companies such as Gallup.

Of course, there is no way to ask all Americans whom they're voting for. So the poll asks a randomly selected group of people whom they would vote for if the election were held that day.

Ideally, the results of the small group reflect the much larger group of US voters. However, in 2016, all the polls were predicting a big Hillary Clinton victory over Donald Trump—and that didn't happen.

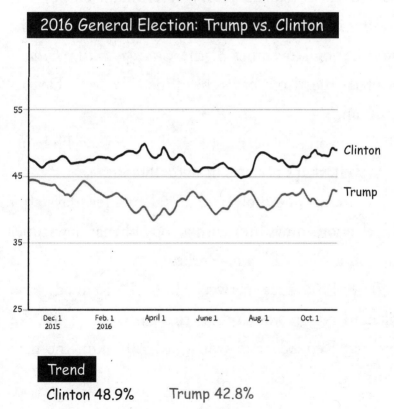

The two lines in the graph track each candidate's popularity in the polls

2016 General Election: Trump vs. Clinton

Clinton

Trump

Dec. 1 2015 Feb. 1 2016 April 1 June 1 Aug. 1 Oct. 1

Trend

Clinton 48.9%   Trump 42.8%

Big upsets, as well as very close calls, have happened before.

On November 2, 1948, it seemed almost certain that a man named Thomas Dewey was going to beat the current president, Harry S. Truman. Dewey was leading in almost every poll. So much so that on the morning of November 3, the *Chicago Daily Tribune* printed the front-page headline "Dewey Defeats Truman."

Have you ever heard of President Dewey? Probably not. Well, that's because he actually lost.

A famous photo of Truman taken a few days after the election shows him with a copy of that newspaper high in the air with a big smile.

The 1960 race between John F. Kennedy and Richard Nixon was so close that NBC News did not say that Kennedy had won until 7:00 a.m. the next morning.

President Harry S. Truman

Track the polls in the weeks leading up to the election. Who conducted the poll? Who does the poll show is leading? By how much?

Date	Name of Poll	Democrat	Republican
Sept 7	_____	☐	☐
Sept 14	_____	☐	☐
Sept 21	_____	☐	☐
Sept 28	_____	☐	☐
Oct 5	_____	☐	☐
Oct 12	_____	☐	☐
Oct 19	_____	☐	☐
Oct 26	_____	☐	☐
Nov 2	_____	☐	☐
(the day before the election)			

Some of the most exciting parts of a presidential race are the debates. There are usually three in the general-election campaign. These debates on TV are way more exciting than all the early primary election debates, because now one of the people onstage will actually become the president.

The debates are conducted by one or more moderators who will ask questions covering different topics. A candidate's answers show how they would govern and how well the candidate thinks on their feet. Often, the candidates get into heated arguments.

Donald Trump and Hillary Clinton in 2016

Donald Trump called Hillary Clinton a "nasty woman" during one debate in 2016. At that same debate, Clinton called Trump a "puppet" of Vladimir Putin, the president of Russia.

A toss of the coin decides who gets the first question. The candidate will have a set amount of time to answer. Their opponent will then have a set amount of time to respond. This is called a rebuttal. Occasionally a candidate will get to make a rebuttal to their opponent's rebuttal.

Candidates will sometimes try to avoid answering a difficult question. They may change the subject or attack their opponent rather than say something the audience might not like. At the end of the debate, each candidate will make a short closing statement repeating why they are the best person to be president.

In recent years, the two vice presidential candidates have also met for one nationally televised debate.

Another form of debate is a "town hall" where members of the audience ask the candidates questions.

The questions also come from people via social media platforms like Facebook and Twitter. During a town hall debate, the candidates move around the room and can address someone in the audience directly. It is always interesting to watch the body language of the candidates. Do they seem confident? Friendly? Nervous?

President Obama and Republican challenger
Mitt Romney in a town hall debate, 2012

You Decide

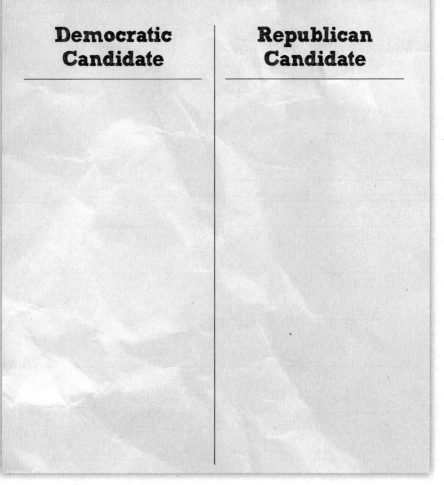

During one of the debates, write down the names of the two candidates. Keep a tally of how many times each tries to avoid answering a question.

Democratic Candidate	Republican Candidate

Rate the Debate

Watch a presidential debate with your family. Then write down your reactions to the candidates. Do you think the candidates are answering the questions or trying to avoid them? Is one trying to attack the other in an unfair way?

DEMOCRAT

_____

_____

_____

_____

_____

_____

_____

Who looks more relaxed? Who seems to better know the issues? Whose answers do you agree with more? At the end of the debate, decide who you think won. See if your family members agree with you.

REPUBLICAN

_____

_____

_____

_____

_____

_____

_____

The First Debate on TV

The first televised presidential debate was on September 26, 1960. Republican candidate Richard Nixon squared off against Democratic candidate John F. Kennedy. Seventy million people tuned in to watch—back then, that was more than one out of every three Americans!

Nixon, who had recently been in the hospital, looked tired and was sweating. He refused to wear any makeup to make himself look better on camera. Even worse, the backdrop behind him was painted the same gray color as his suit, which made him fade into the background. He did not look happy to be there, and he later said that he regretted that he had agreed to the live TV debate.

Kennedy, on the other hand, looked healthy, young, and confident.

Afterward, polls showed that most people who watched the debate on TV thought Kennedy was the clear winner. Many people who listened on the radio, however, thought that Nixon had won the debate. Some historians believe that this debate led to Kennedy's victory in the 1960 election.

From that moment, it was clear that television would change the course of future elections by putting the candidates in view of the US public.

Chapter 11
Election Day

It's finally here! Election Day! The day that all the months of campaigning have led up to, when millions of Americans all across the country will cast their votes for president.

Voting takes place at polling places. Schools, churches, and community centers are often used as polling places.

US citizens must register to vote in advance in most states, but many allow same-day registration. Some states automatically register their residents to vote when they turn eighteen.

In 1848, future President Zachary Taylor didn't cast a ballot for himself. He had never registered to vote!

When voters arrive at the polling place, they check in at a desk. The next stop is the polling booth, where the voting actually takes place. Sometimes there is a long line for the booths, especially for presidential elections.

When a booth is available, the voter goes inside. There are some people who don't decide whom to vote for until this very moment.

Only one adult voter at a time is allowed in each booth so that no one can see whom they vote for. Some states allow kids to accompany grown-ups into the voting booths. Does your state allow this? Ask your parent or guardian if you can come into the booth.

★ ★ ★ ★ ★ ★ ★

Go to the polling place with a grown-up. What was it like? Did you get a sticker? If so, what did it say?

_____

_____

_____

_____

_____

If you could vote in the 2020 election, whom would you choose and why? Did you always support the same person? Or did you change your mind about whom you like better?

_____

_____

_____

_____

_____

★ ★ ★ ★ ★ ★ ★

What if a person can't get to their polling place on Election Day? Perhaps they are going to college in another state, serving in the military overseas, or are not well enough to leave their house. Maybe they have a job and can't get the day off work.

In cases like these, citizens may send in absentee ballots. These are votes cast in advance that sometimes are not counted until after Election Day.

In some states, there is early voting, and people can vote weeks before Election Day. People can also mail in their ballots in certain states.

Polls begin to close in the eastern United States at six o'clock at night. The final polls close in Hawaii seven hours later. Now the votes are tallied.

Take out the map of the United States from the back of your book. As the results are announced throughout Election Night, color in each state red or blue depending on who is declared the winner. Each state on the map shows how many electoral votes it has. Someone may be ahead early in the evening; later on, the other candidate may come from behind as more states report their votes. Since there are a total of 538 electoral votes, a candidate has to get at least 270 to win.

If there ever happens to be a 269–269 tie, then in the House of Representatives, each state casts a single vote and the candidate with a majority wins.

Too Close to Call

The vote in some states might be too close to call right away. In fact, it might take a few hours or even days if the vote is extremely close. In the 2000 election, Democrat Al Gore ran against Republican George W. Bush. It appeared that Gore had won the popular vote. The news networks declared him the winner at first. But then it looked like Bush jumped ahead. Gore even called Bush to admit defeat, or concede.

It turned out, however, that the vote in Florida was too close to award the state's electoral votes. In several districts, people began recounting the ballots. The winner in Florida was not declared until December 12, when the US Supreme Court ordered that the recounts be stopped. In the end, just 537 votes separated the two candidates, and Florida's twenty-five electoral votes went to Bush.

More than a month after Election Day, George W. Bush was declared the winner, with 271 electoral votes versus Gore's 266, although Gore had still won the popular vote by more than half a million votes.

On Election Night, the candidates gather at separate locations with their families and campaign staff, vice presidential running mates, and supporters. They are hoping to celebrate victory, so the rooms are usually decorated with balloons and banners. But they have to be prepared for a loss as well. The room is always full of nervous energy.

Once the results are clear, the candidate who has lost the electoral vote will call the other candidate to admit defeat and congratulate their opponent. They will then make a concession speech to acknowledge their loss publicly. They will thank their staff, who have worked tirelessly for them, as well as their family and supporters throughout the country.

The winner, who is now called the "president-elect," will give an acceptance speech. In 2008, Barack Obama gave his acceptance speech in Chicago's Grant Park. Over 240,000 people attended.

★　　★　　★　　★　　★　　★　　★

Election Day may have come and gone, but it is not the end of the process. We often compare elections to a contest or race, but now that it is over, the real work begins. On January 20, 2021, Inauguration Day, on the steps of the US Capitol, the winner will be sworn into office as the president of the United States.

What kind of president will they be? Will they keep the promises made during the campaign? Will they work with Congress and with members of both parties? Will they make decisions that improve the lives of all US citizens?

Almost right away, preparations will begin for the 2024 presidential election, then 2028 and beyond. Your turn to participate in this important and exciting process is not far away!

Write a Letter

Tell the president-elect what you'd like most to see
happen in the United States over the next four years.
You can send your letter to the White House
by mailing it in a stamped envelope to:

**The White House
1600 Pennsylvania Avenue NW
Washington, DC 20500**

_____

_____

_____

_____

_____

_____

_____

_____

COLOR YOUR OWN ELE[CTION]
Blue for Democrats •

Follow along on Election
270 electoral votes—

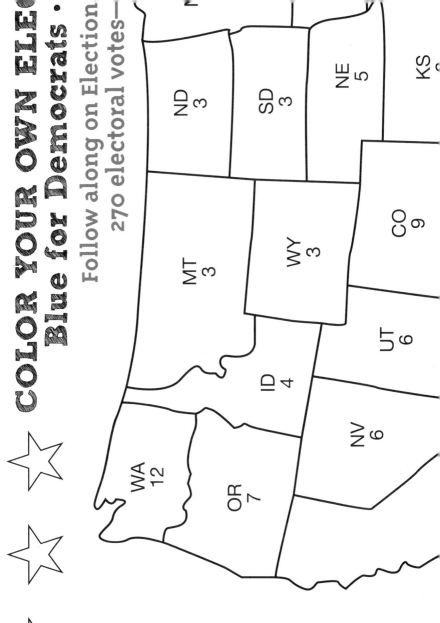

WA
12

OR
7

ID
4

MT
3

ND
3

SD
3

NE
5

WY
3

NV
6

UT
6

CO
9

KS

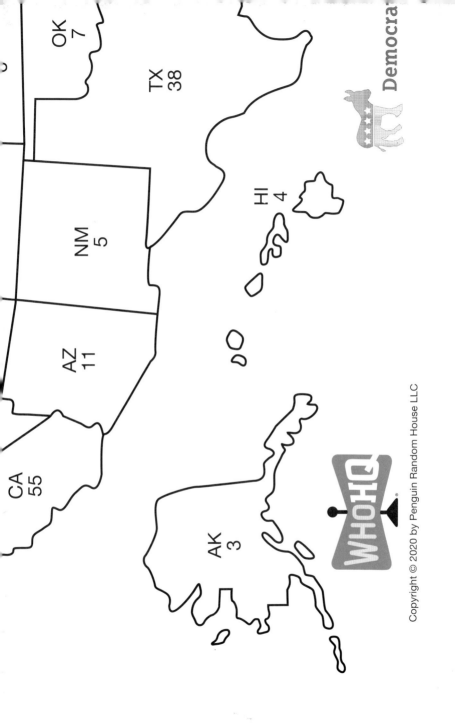

OK
7

TX
38

NM
5

HI
4

AZ
11

CA
55

AK
3

Democrat